THE TRADINGWINDOWS STRATEGY

By

The Connors Research Group

M. Gordon Publishing Group, Inc.

Los Angeles, California

Copyright (c) 2002 by Laurence A. Connors.

ALL RIGHTS RESERVED. No part of this publication may be reproduced, stored in a retrieval system, or transmitted, in any form or by any means, electronic, mechanical, photocopying, recording, or otherwise, without the prior written permission of the publisher and the authors.

This publication is designed to provide accurate and authoritative information in regard to the subject matter covered. It is sold with the understanding that the authors and the publisher are not engaged in rendering legal, accounting, or other professional service.

Authorization to photocopy items for internal or personal use, or in the internal or personal use of specific clients, is granted by M. Gordon Publishing Group, Inc., provided that the U.S. $7.00 per page fee is paid directly to M. Gordon Publishing Group, Inc., 1-213-955-5777.

ISBN 1-893756-14-9

Printed in the United States of America

Performance tables contained in this book were created with TradeStation2000i by TradeStation Technologies, Inc. TradeStation is a registered trademark of TradeStation Technologies, Inc.

As indicated, charts used in this book are Copyright © 2002 Bloomberg LP. Reprinted with permission. All rights reserved.

Disclaimer

It should not be assumed that the methods, techniques, or indicators presented in these products will be profitable or that they will not result in losses. Past results are not necessarily indicative of future results. Examples presented in this book are for educational purposes only. These setups are not solicitations of any order to buy or sell. The authors, the publisher, and all affiliates assume no responsibility for your trading results. There is a high degree of risk in trading.

The NFA requires us to state that "HYPOTHETICAL OR SIMULATED PERFORMANCE RESULTS HAVE CERTAIN INHERENT LIMITATIONS. UNLIKE AN ACTUAL PERFORMANCE RECORD, SIMULATED RESULTS DO NOT REPRESENT ACTUAL TRADING. ALSO, SINCE THE TRADES HAVE NOT ACTUALLY BEEN EXECUTED, THE RESULTS MAY HAVE UNDER- OR OVER-COMPENSATED FOR THE IMPACT, IF ANY, OF CERTAIN MARKET FACTORS, SUCH AS LACK OF LIQUIDITY. SIMULATED TRADING PROGRAMS IN GENERAL ARE ALSO SUBJECT TO THE FACT THAT THEY ARE DESIGNED WITH THE BENEFIT OF HINDSIGHT. NO REPRESENTATION IS BEING MADE THAT ANY ACCOUNT WILL OR IS LIKELY TO ACHIEVE PROFITS OR LOSSES SIMILAR TO THOSE SHOWN."

Table of Contents

Introduction	7
Part One—What is a "TradingWindow"?	9
Part Two—TradingWindows: Rules and Variations	15
Part Three—Exit Strategies	27
Part Four—Real-World Situations	37
Q&A	56
Conclusion	62
Appendix	64

Introduction

Over the past decade, I have been researching price movement and market timing almost continuously. A good deal of my research in the mid-90s focused on the role that ADX and ±DI (Directional Index) play in price continuation. For those of you who do not know, ADX measures the persistency of a trend. The higher the ADX, and/or ±DI, the stronger the trend. *In my opinion, nothing measures trend better (all this will be fully explained in the next chapter).* I have also found that for many strategies, simply adding ADX and/or ±DI as a filter to a strategy immediately increases the performance of that strategy.

My other focus over the past year has been on the role that the VIX plays in predicting short-term market direction. This research has now grown extensively and it remains the core of my market timing strategies. The key aspect behind the VIX and all volatility is that it reverts to its mean. That means high periods of volatility will eventually revert to lower volatility and low periods of volatility will eventually be followed by higher periods of volatility. These reversions are usually accompanied by stock market prices reversing to previous levels. (See "Trading Connors VIX Reversals" and "Buy The Fear, Sell The Greed".)

One of the natural questions I have asked is that if volatility reverts to its mean, does that mean that prices also revert to their mean? The academic world has proven conclusively that volatility does revert to its mean but there are fewer studies that prove it with price. The studies that are out there tend to be focused on

very long-term periods, i.e., months or years, and this does little for traders.

In my opinion, prices do revert to their mean but they occur more selectively than volatility. They tend to revert to their mean after trending strongly and then have a move that sharply goes against this trend. There are many strategies that have been published that show this (I've published a handful myself) but, in my opinion, none does it better than when a market trades in a pattern that I call a **"TradingWindow."** In this book, I will teach you how to find these "Windows," how to enter them and how to best exit your positions. The method is fairly simple and combines two of the strongest elements available to traders, ADX and/or ±DI, along with price reversals in the direction of the longer-term trend.

Part One

What is a "TradingWindow"? It is simply a strongly trending market that has pulled away from a short-term simple moving average. **The space in between the moving average is the "Window."**

Figure 2.1—Semiconductor HOLDRs Trust (SMH)—Daily

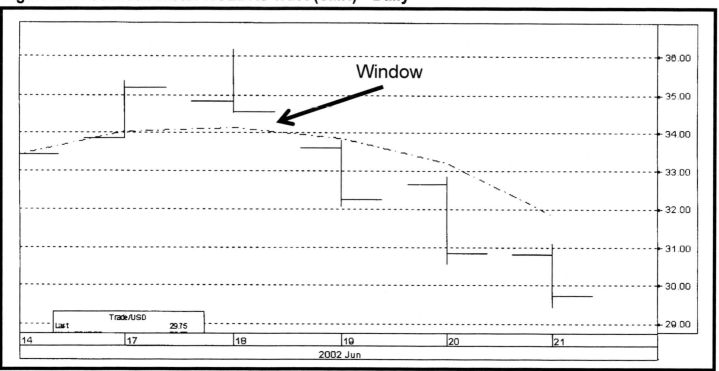

Figure 2.1 — The low of the daily bar is above the 4-period moving average. This space between the moving average and the low is known as a "Window."

There are 5 types of Windows. These are *GapWindows*, *DoubleWindows*, *AggressiveWindows*, *HangingWindows*, and the most common, *SingleWindows*. The SingleWindows will occur the majority of the time and are the backbone of the strategy. GapWindows occur the least but they are the most powerful.

Before we look at the various Windows, let's first look at the role trend plays in trading a Window. Obviously, markets trend. And the very best way to identify and measure a trend is with ADX and/or the Directional Indicator known as ±DI.

ADX simply measures the strength of the trend, not its direction. The stronger the trend, the higher the ADX. An ADX reading above 20 tells you the market is in a good trend. An ADX reading above 30 tells you it's in a solid trend. In order to identify the best "TradingWindows," **we want the stock or market we are trading to have an ADX reading of 30 or higher.**

The component of the ADX that measures the direction and also measures the strength of the trend is the +DI and –DI. If the trend is up, the +DI will be greater than the –DI. If the trend is down, the –DI will be greater than the +DI (all this will be simple to understand once you see more charts). The stronger the trend up, the higher the +DI will be. The stronger the trend down, the higher the –DI will be.

Figure 2.2—Nasdaq 100 Index (NDX)—Daily

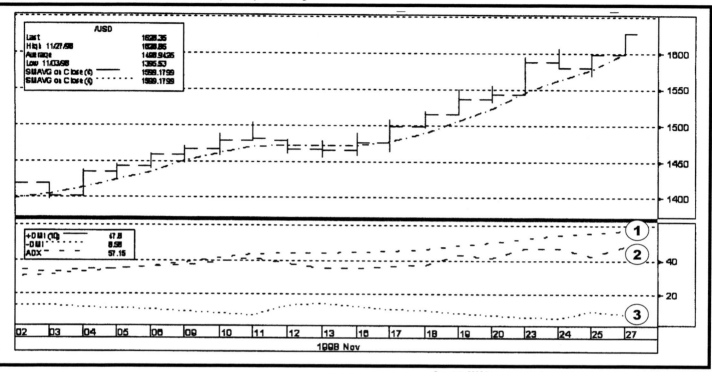

The trend is up.

1) The ADX is ≥ 30, signifying a strong trend.

2) & 3) The +DI is > -DI, signifying an uptrend.

In order for us to be a buyer of a "TradingWindow," we must have a 10-period ADX reading of 30 or higher and a +DI reading above the –DI reading. Or we must have a 14-period +DI of 30 or higher (with no ADX reading required). In order for us to have a sell signal, the 10-period ADX must be 30 or higher and the –DI must be greater than the +DI. Or, we must have a 14-period –DI reading of above 30 (with no ADX reading required).

Those are the only rules we require for measuring the trend. Now, let's look at the Windows patterns. As I mentioned, we want to identify stocks (or futures) that have moved away from a simple moving average. **That means that on an uptrend, the high of today's price is below its moving average. For a downtrending stock, the low of the day must be above its moving average.**

And which moving averages do I use? A 4-day simple moving average. Why 4 days? Because for a stock to not touch its 4-day MA today, it must have moved well away from its normal, short-term trend. And for it to move well beyond its short-term trend is the potential beginning of a market that has a likelihood of "snapping back" in the direction of its very strong longer-term trend.

Let's look at a market that shows itself moving away from its short-term moving average before reversing.

Figure 2.3—Nasdaq 100 Tracking Stock (QQQ)—Daily

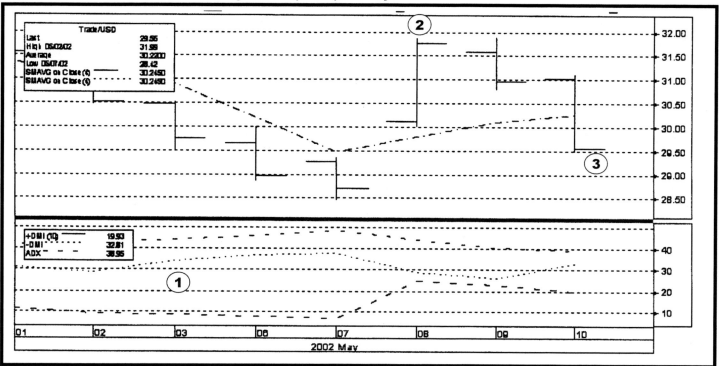

1) The trend is down as the ADX is greater than 30 and the –DI is greater than the +DI.

2) Two Window setups as both days are above their 4-day moving average.

3) A reversal back through the moving average and back to its longer-term trend.

Notes

Part Two

Rules And Variations

As you will see, there are only a small number of times when a market doesn't touch its 4-day simple moving average. The majority of the time it trades through the moving average and is "Windowless." Now, before going on, I will tell you that "TradingWindows" occur with other moving averages. You can use a higher moving average (5-day MA, 6-day MA, etc.) and get more trades that are a bit less reliable or you can use a 3-day moving average and get fewer trades. For me, 4-days seems to work best and is the time period we will use throughout this book.

Now let's look at the 5 different types of "Windows."

SingleWindows

SingleWindows are the most common type of Windows. They are simply a single bar which has its low trading above the 4-period moving average or its high of the day below the 4-period moving average. You will enter tomorrow if the market trades above today's high (for buys) or below today's low (for sells).

Here is an example of a SingleWindow.

Figure 3.1—Pharmaceutical HOLDRs Trust (PPH)—Daily

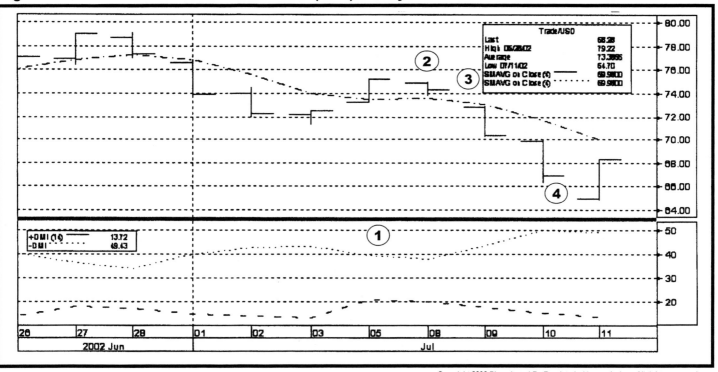

Copyright 2002 Bloomberg LP. Reprinted with permission. All rights reserved.

1) The 14-period -DI is above 30. This signifies the trend is down.

2) The Pharmaceutical HOLDRs trade above their 4-period simple moving average for the entire day, creating a Window setup.

3) The PPHs trade under the July 8 low, triggering a sell signal.

4) They proceed to lose 10% of their value through the next day.

DoubleWindows

A "DoubleWindow" is two "SingleWindows" in a row. This setup obviously occurs less often than SingleWindows. The entry is the same as a SingleWindow. You will enter uptrending stocks on the buy side if tomorrow trades above today's high and you will enter downtrending stocks on the short side tomorrow if it trades under today's low. Here is an example of a "DoubleWindow" buy.

Figure 3.2—Broker Dealer Index (XBD)—Daily

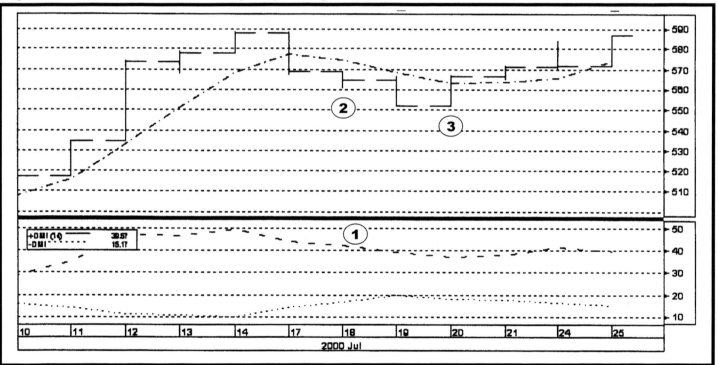

Copyright 2002 Bloomberg LP. Reprinted with permission. All rights reserved.

1) The 14-period +DI is greater than 30. The trend is up.

2) Two Windows in a row as both days trade under their 4-period moving average.

3) Enter long on July 20 as it takes out the previous day's high.

Both SingleWindows and DoubleWindows have you entering the next day only if the market resumes its move in the direction of the trend. The next 3 Window setups have you entering either your choice of the next day or on the day they occur. Let's go through what these setups are and then we'll discuss in further depth the entries.

AggressiveWindows

"AggressiveWindows" are exactly as they sound, aggressive! For sell setups, they are single or double Windows that close in the bottom 5% of their daily range and close below their open. For buys, they close in the top 5% of their daily range and above the open. What makes this aggressive is that instead of waiting for the next day for the market to take out its high or low, *you are buying on the close today in the direction of the trend*. This means you are betting that the reversion to the mean has already begun and you are front running tomorrow's move. Many times, when you are right, you will see tomorrow's open gap in the direction of your position. The drawback is that because you are not waiting for tomorrow's follow through confirmation, <u>you will be wrong more than normal</u>. This is a personal choice of yours whether or not to enter on the close of the day or wait for the next day to confirm the move.

Here is an example of AggressiveWindows

Figure 3.3—Broker Dealer Index (XBD)—Daily

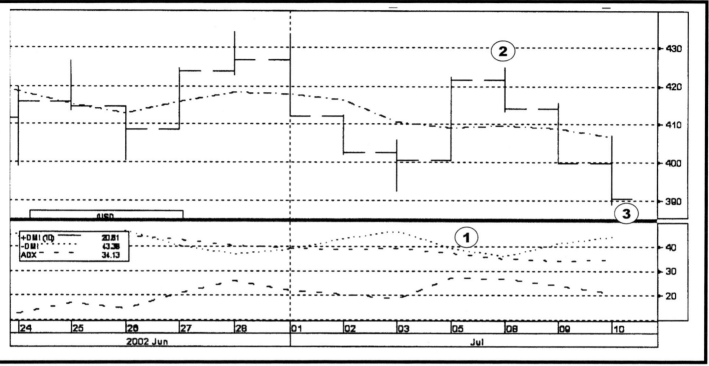

1) ADX is above 30 and the –DI > +DI. The trend is down.

2) AggressiveWindow as it closes in the bottom 5% of the range and the close is below the open. The short will take place on the close. (Please note that you cannot trade the XBDs outright. This example is being shown for its chart pattern.)

3) Prices collapse.

HangingWindows

HangingWindows occur when a market or stock opens and closes in the bottom 10% of its daily range for sells and in the top 10% of its daily range for buys. They look like this:

<u>Buys</u>

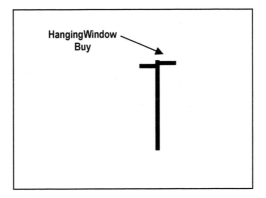

<u>Sells</u>

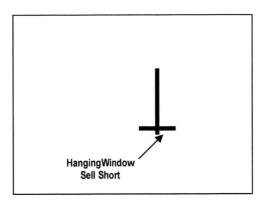

They should be entered on the close but if you miss them, then you can enter on the opening the next day. The key to this setup is understanding that the market (for buys) is in a strong uptrend. The stock traded today under its 4-day moving average but its intraday sell-off fails and a rally occurs. For short sales, the opposite is happening. The stock is strongly downtrending as measured by ADX and/or ±DI. It then jumps higher but fails to hold its rally, setting itself up for a resumption of the trend. Here is an example of a HangingWindow on KLAC.

Figure 3.4—KLA-Tencor Corp. (KLAC)—Daily

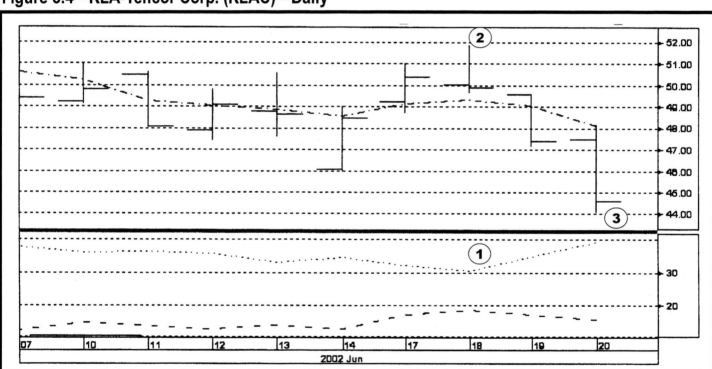

Copyright 2002 Bloomberg LP. Reprinted with permission. All rights reserved.

1) The 14-period -DI is greater than 30, signifying a downtrend.

2) KLAC opens and closes in the bottom 10% of its daily range and trades the entire day above the 4-period moving average. Sell short on the close.

3) Stock drops 10% in 2 days.

GapWindows

The final Window setup is "GapWindows." They occur the least often of the Windows setups but they perform among the best.

There are two types of GapWindows, one that triggers intraday and the other that triggers at the close. Let's look at the intraday entry first.

The rules for the intraday entry are as follows for Buys:

1) As with all the Windows, you must have a 10-period ADX $\geq$ 30 and its +DI > -DI, or a 14-period +DI by itself that is greater than or equal to 30. Also, yesterday must be a SingleWindow or DoubleWindow day.

2) If today gaps open below yesterday's low, we buy at yesterday's low.

For Sells

1) ADX $\geq$ 30, -DI > +DI, or a 14-period –DI by itself that is greater than or equal to 30. Also, yesterday must be either a SingleWindow or DoubleWindow day.

2) If today gaps open above yesterday's high, we sell at yesterday's high.

Here is an example of a GapWindow.

Figure 3.5—Biotech HOLDRs Trust (BBH)—Intraday

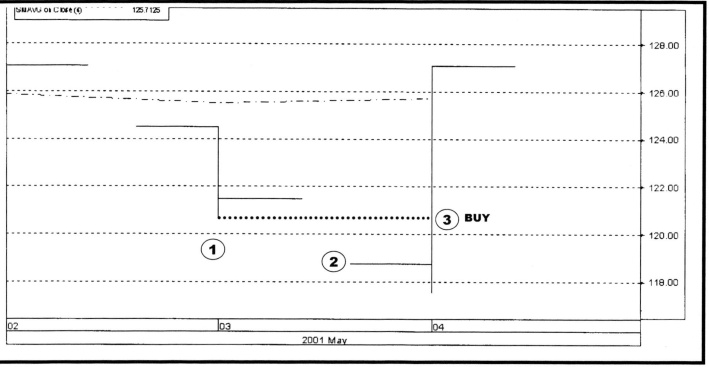

1) BBH creates a window pattern because its high is below the 4-day moving average and the trend is up.

2) Gap opening lower.

3) Buy at yesterday's low.

Close Of The Day GapWindows

Close Of The Day GapWindows simply have a strong trend that gaps in the opposite direction, closes above its open for buys (below its open for sells), and makes a Window. We buy on the close when this occurs. Here is an example.

Figure 3.6—Juniper Networks (JNPR)—Daily

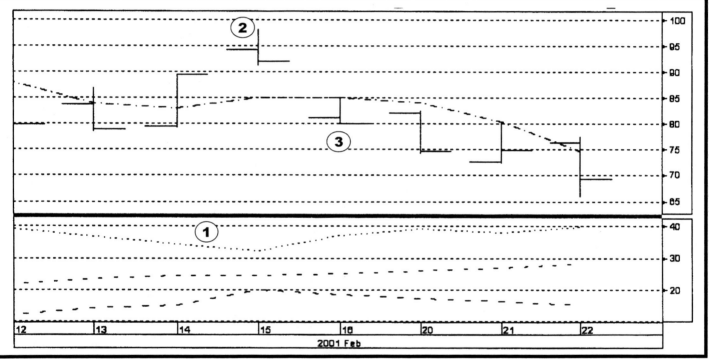

Copyright 2002 Bloomberg LP. Reprinted with permission. All rights reserved.

1) Trend is down as the –DI > 30.

2) GapWindow, sell on the close.

3) Gaps nearly 9 points lower the next morning. Though this pattern is fairly rare, it is among the most powerful out there.

The reason why we trade the gaps at the close instead of the following day is that in many cases, the rubber band has been pulled (with the gap) and the strong close tells us that there is a higher-than-normal likelihood that the trend will resume.

Now that you are armed with entry for the 5 Windows setups, let's now move on to the exit strategies.

Notes

Part Three

Exit Strategies

The exit strategies for the TradingWindows are far less mechanical than the entries. We'll first look at protective stops for the trades and then we will look at profit-taking strategies.

Protective Stops

The initial protective stops for the SingleWindows and DoubleWindows are at the bottom/top of the previous day's bar. This means that if there was a Single or DoubleWindow buy setup yesterday, and we enter today, our protective stop will be at the bottom of yesterday's bar. If yesterday there was a single or double Window setup on the short side and we entered today, our stop would be at the top of yesterday's bar. These types of stops keep our losses small while allowing us to be in positions that have a solid likelihood of moving in our favor, many times substantially.

Figure 4.1—Baxter International (BAX)—Daily

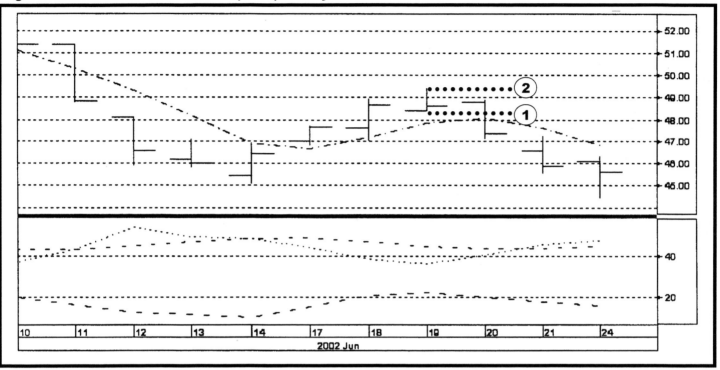

1) A short entry on a SingleWindow formation.

2) The initial protective stop is at the high of Window day.

The protective stops for AggressiveWindows, HangingWindows and on the close GapWindows are basically the same but because we are entering on the close, our stop is at the bottom of today's bar for buys and at the top of today's bar for sells.

Here is an example.

Figure 4.2—Internet HOLDRs Trust (HHH)—Daily

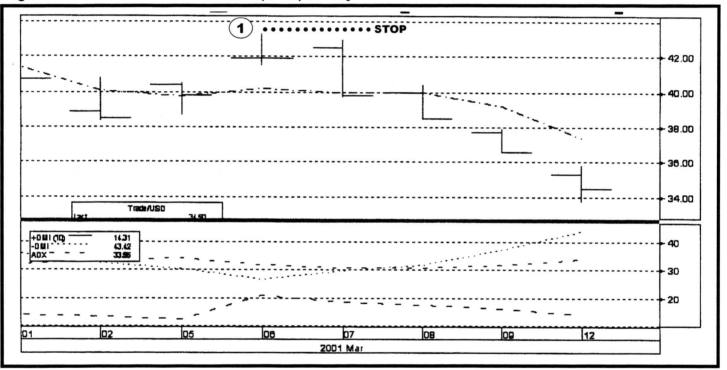

Copyright 2002 Bloomberg LP. Reprinted with permission. All rights reserved.

1) Here is an example of a very successful HangingWindow. We go short on the close of March 6 and our stop is at the high of the day.

For intraday GapWindows, our stop for long positions is either today's open or today's low (your choice for buys). For short positions, our stop is either today's open or today's high (your choice). Here is an example.

Figure 4.3—Amazon.com (AMZN)—Daily

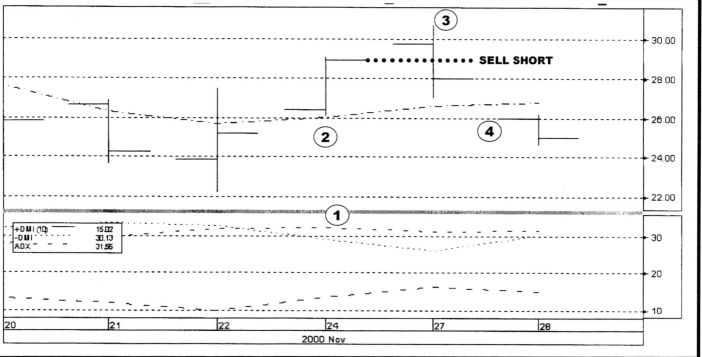

Copyright 2002 Bloomberg LP. Reprinted with permission. All rights reserved.

1) The trend is down in Amazon.com: ADX > 30 and the −DI > +DI.

2) Low is just above the 4-day moving average, creating a Window.

3) Short at yesterday's high of 29.12 and our protective stop is at the high today of 30.31.

4) Gaps lower to 26 into the opening.

Taking Profits

Taking profits is the area in which you will have the most discretion. Most of the time, you will be exiting in 1-4 days. What you do not know, is just how far or just how long a move will go. Therefore, we're going to combine a reversion-to-the-mean exit along with a trailing stop exit.

A reversion-to-the-mean exit means we exit 1/4 to 1/3 our position when the market closes above its 4-day simple moving average for buys, or below its 4-day simple moving average for sells. At the same time we exit, we will move our stop on the remaining 1/2 to 3/4 of our position to breakeven.

For example, if we buy today a stock at 35, and yesterday's low was 34.25, we will have our protective stop at 34.25 on our entire position. Let's say the stock closes at 36 and the SMA today closes at 35.42, we will exit 1/4 to 1/3 our position at the close or at the opening the next day. Upon being filled, we will move our stop to 35 (our entry) on the remaining pieces, guaranteeing us a profitable trade (barring some crazy overnight event).

From this point, we will use trailing stops. That means that as the position moves further in our favor, we move our stops higher (for buys) and lower (for sells). At the same time, we will look to "piece out," meaning exit, a piece more as prices move higher. Let's continue with the same example. Our stock goes up to 37; we'll sell another piece off and move our stop on the remaining piece to the 36.25 – 36.50 range. Discretion, market strength/weakness, etc., will help you decide how to proceed here. And if the market continues to run, you can sell a piece more or simply exit completely. The goal is to allow the market to move in your favor and as it is doing this, profitably exit partial amounts of your position. Remember, you are trading a strongly moving stock in the direction of the trend and

you want to take advantage of this trend as it resumes.

To give you an idea of the strength of this strategy, and the wisdom of exiting after we move above/below the moving average, I have added a few test results here. Please note: These are mechanical, single rule exits and I do not trade Windows in this manner. **They are simply here to show you the potential effectiveness of this strategy.** They are also shown to those of you who like to create mechanical systems to trade. If you are one of these people, there is much you can do here.

These two tests have only two rules. You exit if the second day is not profitable or if it closes above/below the 4-day moving average two days in a row. Again, I do not trade mechanically, but these are shown as examples to point to the strategy's potential.

US T.Bond-CBT-Daily   01/05/1990 - 09/09/2002

Performance Summary: All Trades

Total net profit	$16312.50	Open position P/L	0.00
Gross profit	22781.25	Gross loss	-6468.75
Total # of trades	47	Percent profitable	(81%)
Number winning trades	38	Number losing trades	9
Largest winning trade	2093.75	Largest losing trade	-1656.25
Average winning trade	599.51	Average losing trade	-718.75
Ratio avg win/avg loss	0.83	Avg trade(win & loss)	347.07
Max consec. winners	7	Max consec. losers	2
Avg # bars in winners	1	Avg # bars in losers	2
Max intraday drawdown	-1843.75		
Profit factor	3.52	Max # contracts held	1
Account size required	1843.75	Return on account	885%

Performance Summary: Long Trades

Total net profit	11562.50	Open position P/L	0.00
Gross profit	15312.50	Gross loss	-3750.00
Total # of trades	32	Percent profitable	81%
Number winning trades	26	Number losing trades	6
Largest winning trade	1437.50	Largest losing trade	-1562.50
Average winning trade	588.94	Average losing trade	-625.00
Ratio avg win/avg loss	0.94	Avg trade(win & loss)	361.33
Max consec. winners	6	Max consec. losers	1
Avg # bars in winners	1	Avg # bars in losers	2
Max intraday drawdown	-1718.75		
Profit factor	4.08	Max # contracts held	1
Account size required	1718.75	Return on account	673%

Performance Summary: Short Trades

Total net profits	4750.00	Open position P/L	0.00
Gross profit	7468.75	Gross loss	-2718.75
Total # of trades	15	Percent profitable	80%
Number winning trades	12	Number losing trades	3
Largest winning trade	2093.75	Largest losing trade	-1656.25
Average winning trade	622.40	Average losing trade	-906.25
Ratio avg win/avg loss	0.69	Avg trade(win & loss)	316.67
Max consec. Winners	5	Max consec. losers	1
Avg # bars in winners	1	Avg # bars in losers	2
Max intraday drawdown	-1843.75		
Profit factor	2.75	Max # contracts held	1
Account size required	1843.75	Return on account	258%

The TradingWindows Strategy

AMEX Broker/Dealer Index-Daily   04/15/1994 - 09/11/2002

Performance Summary: All Trades

Total net profit	392.99 points	Open position P/L	0.00
Gross profit	578.17	Gross loss	-185.18
Total # of trades	103	Percent profitable	64%
Number winning trades	66	Number losing trades	37
Largest winning trade	50.73	Largest losing trade	-30.20
Average winning trade	8.76	Average losing trade	-5.00
Ratio avg win/avg loss	1.75	Avg trade(win & loss)	3.82
Max consec. winners	11	Max consec. losers	5
Avg # bars in winners	1	Avg # bars in losers	1
Max intraday drawdown	-59.36		
Profit factor	3.12	Max # contracts held	1
Account size required	59.36	Return on account	662%

Performance Summary: Long Trades

Total net profit	216.90	Open position P/L	0.00
Gross profit	294.28	Gross loss	-77.38
Total # of trades	67	Percent profitable	70%
Number winning trades	47	Number losing trades	20
Largest winning trade	50.73	Largest losing trade	-18.34
Average winning trade	6.26	Average losing trade	-3.87
Ratio avg win/avg loss	1.62	Avg trade(win & loss)	3.24
Max consec. winners	11	Max consec. losers	3
Avg # bars in winners	1	Avg # bars in losers	1
Max intraday drawdown	-33.35		
Profit factor	3.80	Max # contracts held	1
Account size required	33.35	Return on account	650%

Performance Summary: Short Trades

Total net profit	176.09	Open position P/L	0.00
Gross profit	283.89	Gross loss	-107.80
Total # of trades	36	Percent profitable	53%
Number winning trades	19	Number losing trades	17
Largest winning trade	34.19	Largest losing trade	-30.20
Average winning trade	14.94	Average losing trade	-6.34
Ratio avg win/avg loss	2.36	Avg trade(win & loss)	4.89
Max consec. winners	4	Max consec. Losers	5
Avg # bars in winners	1	Avg # bars in losers	1
Max intraday drawdown	-39.03		
Profit factor	2.63	Max # contracts held	1
Account size required	39.03	Return on account	451%

Let's now look to some real world examples. We'll look at the entire TradingWindows process. This means identification, entry, protective stops, partial and full profit taking, and many nuances of the strategies.

Notes

Part Four

Real-World Situations

I'm now going to walk you through 17 different Windows situations. These situations are shown to help you further understand the Windows strategy. After we look at these situations, we'll wrap things up with a handful of questions and answers. By the time you are finished with the Q&A section, you should be able to start applying Windows to your trading immediately.

Situation 1

The Perfect Window

Figure 5.1—Merrill Lynch (MER)—Daily

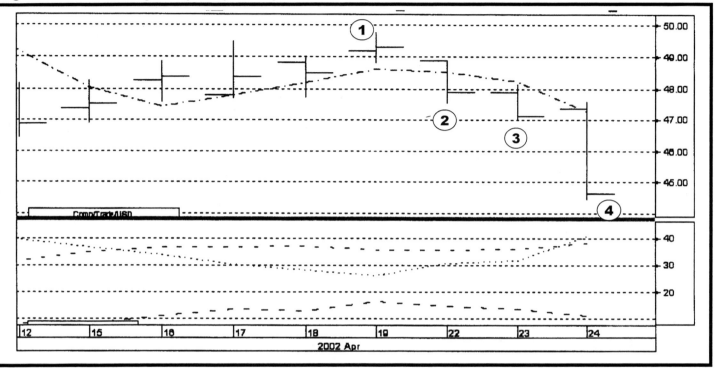

Copyright 2002 Bloomberg LP. Reprinted with permission. All rights reserved.

The "PerfectWindow" will give you 3 solid days of profits. Such a pattern exists as you see it above.

1) Trend is down and a SingleWindow formation.

2) A short entry and a good first day profit. Taking profits on a small piece on the close, especially after it closes well under its 4-day moving average, and moving your stop to breakeven on the remainder of your position is proper trade management.

3) More profits on the second day and we'll be taking additional gains off the table again.

4) A large move for us and final profits will be locked in. I've found that 3 days is an optimal time to lock in your final gains.

Situation 2

Another Perfect Window

Figure 5.2—Semiconductor HOLDRs Trust (SMH)—Daily

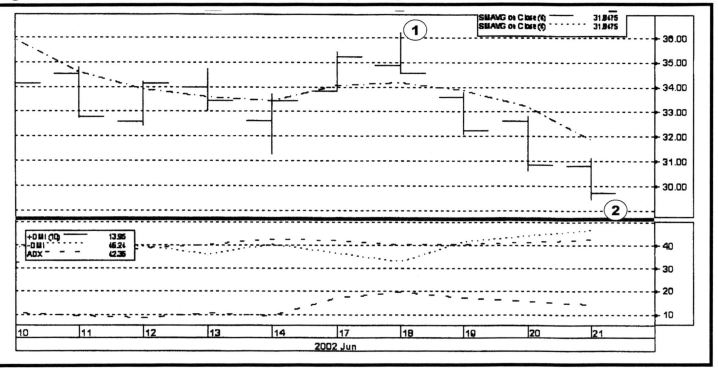

1&2 — Another example of a "PerfectWindow." Here it's also an AggressiveWindow setup. **Please note:** You can also enter on the short side the next morning if it takes out the Window day low. This is a more conservative strategy.

Situation 3

Getting Stopped Out

Figure 5.3—Broker Dealer Index (XBD)—Daily

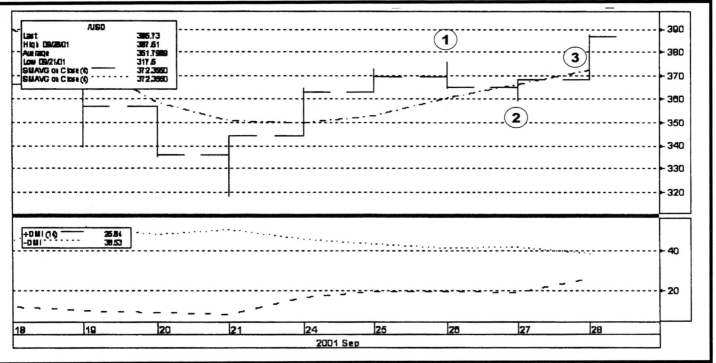

Obviously, getting stopped out of a position is the opposite of a Perfect Window. It will happen all the time. The key is to stay disciplined. Because the Windows lend such a solid edge, taking small losses is part of the strategy, as is taking the gains that occur when the setup works. You'll see many small losses and many small gains along with a handful of outsize gains (also see the Q&A section).

1) Here is an example of what it looks like to get stopped out. We have a DoubleWindow sell.

2) A small profit intraday that then reverses.

3) We get stopped out at the high of the Window bar.

Situation 4

A Window That Works For 1 1/2 Days

Figure 5.4—Oracle Corp. (ORCL)—Daily

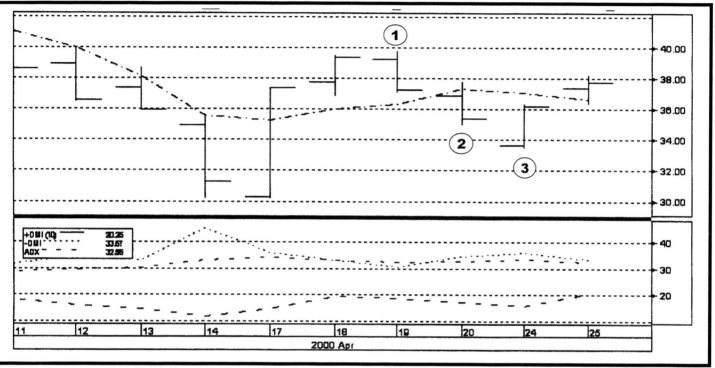

Copyright 2002 Bloomberg LP. Reprinted with permission. All rights reserved.

1) Here's an AggressiveDoubleWindow that is successful for 1 1/2 days before it reverses. Your success trading the Windows will be predicated by your trade management in these situations. You must be locking in profits along the way in order to maximize the success of the strategy.

2) One-quarter to one-third of the profits must be taken, the stock has closed well under its 4-day moving average.

3) When this gap begins to reverse, your profit-taking needs to become aggressive. You cannot allow good gains to turn into small gains or worse, a loss. At this point, more profits will likely be locked in around 35-35.25 and I'd for sure be out of the final piece on the next day's gap opening. THERE IS NO MECHANICAL SCIENCE TO THIS. MARKETS CAN AND WILL DO A THOUSAND VARIATIONS OF MOVEMENT AND THE CORRECT WAY TO TRADE IS TO BE LOCKING IN PIECES AND PUTTING IT IN YOUR BANK ACCOUNT.

Situation 5

No Gain First Day

Figure 5.5—Goldman Sachs Group Inc. (GS)—Daily

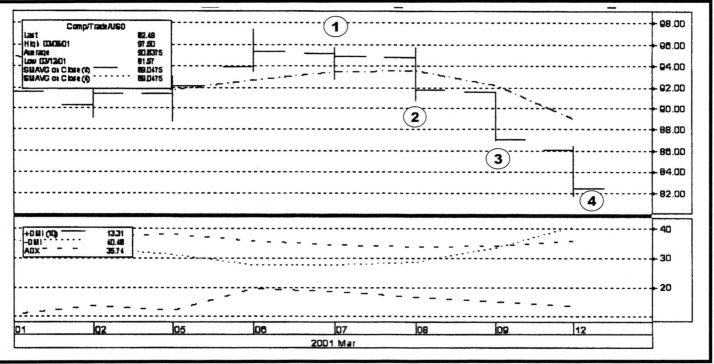

If you do not have a profit the first day and have not been stopped out, there is no reason to do anything.

1) A SingleWindow entry but it closes the day with a small loss. There is no reason to exit the trade, nor move your stop.

2) The first day that it closes under the 4-day moving average and is also a pretty good profit. Start locking in profits by covering a piece of your short position.

3) Lock in more profits.

4) Lock in more profits.

Situation 6

Trading Other Markets

Figure 5.6—Gold Futures (GCM2)—Daily

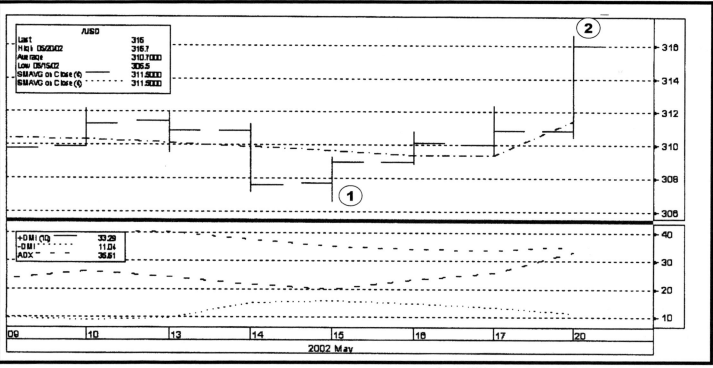

In my opinion, if a pattern works in one market, it should work in all markets. The next 3 situations help bring this out. Gold, coffee, and bonds are very different markets, yet they exhibit the same behavior with a Window setup.

Situation 7

Other Markets Continued

Figure 5.7—Coffee Futures (KCZ0)—Daily

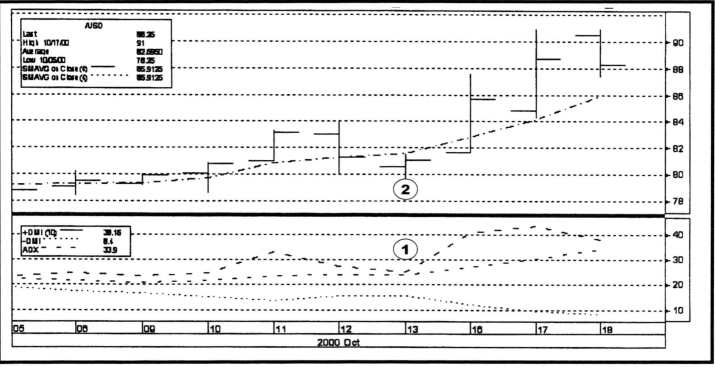

1) Trend is up.

2) High is just under the 4-period moving average, creating a Window setup before Coffee prices explode higher.

Situation 8

More Other Markets

Figure 5.8—US Bond Futures (USU2)—Daily

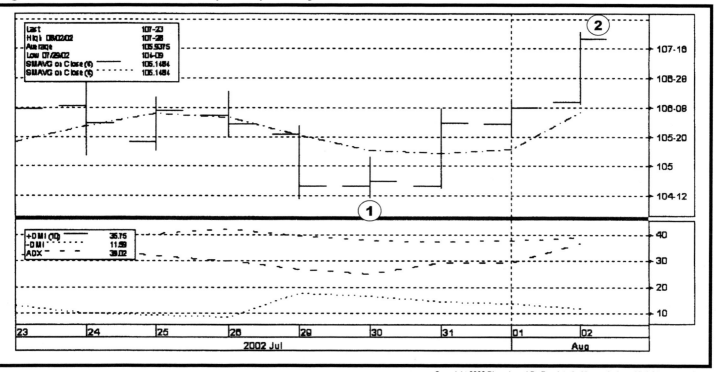

1 & 2 — Another example of the "PerfectWindow." These consecutive days of profits with the third day exploding higher, this time in Bonds.

Situation 9

Triple Windows

Figure 5.9—Semiconductor Holdrs Trust (SMH)—Daily

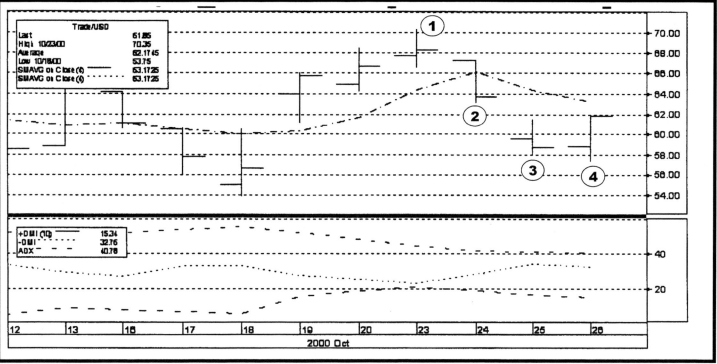

You trade TripleWindows no different than any other Windows.

1) Here is a "TripleWindow" and the same entry holds.

2) Short and a good first day profit that closes under the 4-day. Take some profits here. Move the remaining position to breakeven.

3) A gap lower and a chance to lock in further profits during the day.

4) Your profits are diminishing during the day on the final piece. Trailing stops will assure that the profits are locked in.

Situation 10

Gap Openings On The Other Side Of The Moving Average

Figure 5.10—Qlogic Corp. (QLGC)—Daily

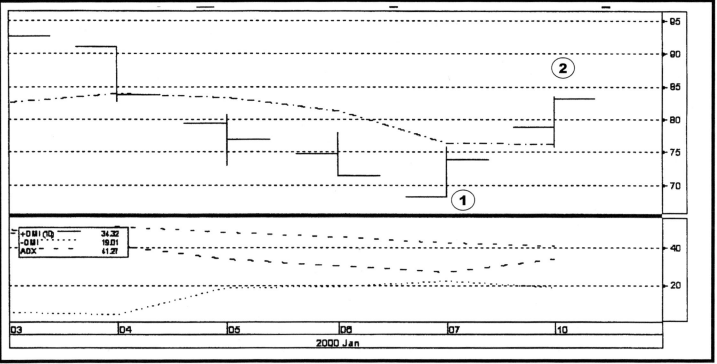

Many times you will have a Window setup that gaps open the next morning in the direction of the longer-term trend. You may believe the move is now over, but I have found that more often than not, it is just the beginning of the move.

1) A "Triple Window."

2) When the market gaps above the 4-day moving average, it's still a buy, but you will want to raise your initial stop higher in this situation, likely to the Window day close.

Situation 11

AggressiveWindows

Figure 5.11—SPDRs Trust (SPY)—Daily

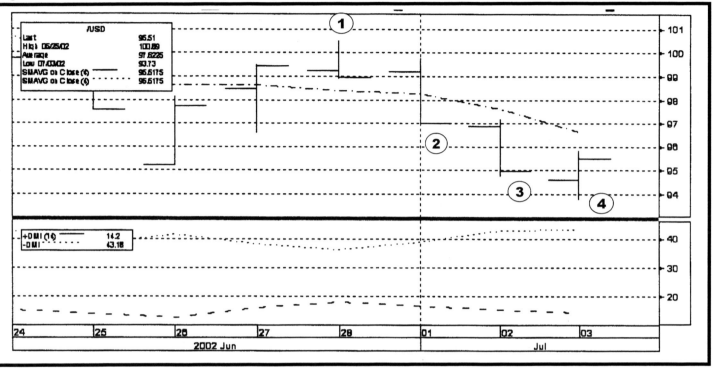

I only recommend you trade AggressiveWindows if you are very risk-oriented. They many times lead to solid overnight gains, but they are also wrong more than average. This is your own personal choice whether to trade them or wait until the next day.

1) An AggressiveWindow at 99.

2) Some profits can be taken at 97 near the close and the remaining piece moves to 99 on the protective stop.

3) More profits to lock in.

4) The final piece can be locked in.

Situation 12

More Trade Management

Figure 5.12—Juniper Networks (JNPR)—Daily

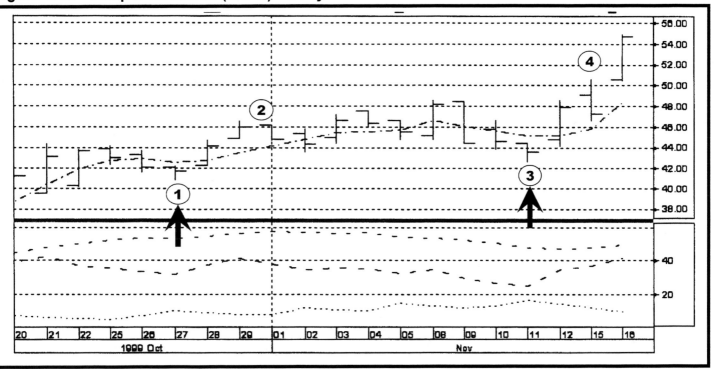

1 & 2) The first of two Window trades. You need to become very aggressive in your profit taking when it starts reversing November 1.

3) Another Window.

4) Tricky. You need to be locking in gains here. I'd be locking in all my gains on this bar. The next day's rally does not happen often but when it does, you just need to ignore it. You had a good profitable gain and your bank account will be far better off in the long run by being aggressive in taking gains. This is real world trading.

Situation 13

More Trade Management

Figure 5.13—10-Year T-Note Futures (TYU2)—Daily

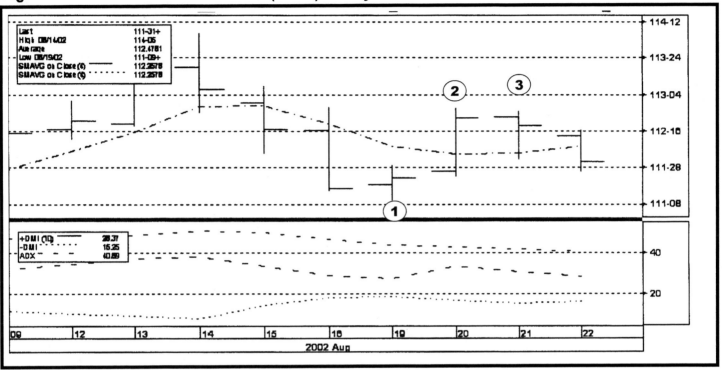

1) A SingleWindow.

2) Profit-taking on a piece and move your stop to breakeven.

3) Intraday weakness and again you'll be using discretion as to how aggressive you want to be in locking in all your gains.

Situation 14

Size of the Window

Figure 5.14—Freddie Mac (FRE)—Daily

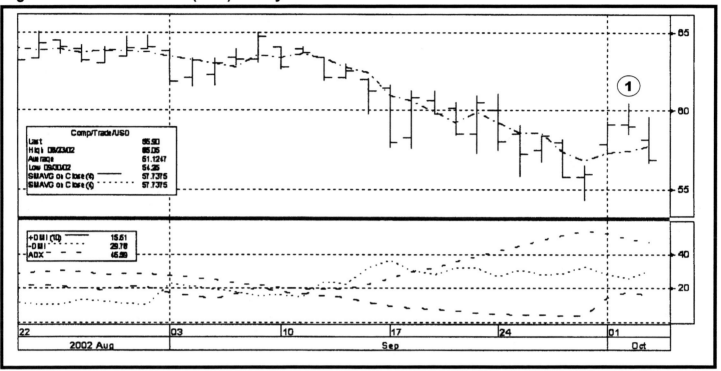

1) On nights that you have "too many windows," you may want to look for those with "large" Windows. In the above example, look at the space between FRE and the moving average. It's significant and it has more travel room before it reverts to its moving average.

Situation 15

Large First Day Gains

Figure 5.15—Whirlpool Corp. (WHR)—Daily

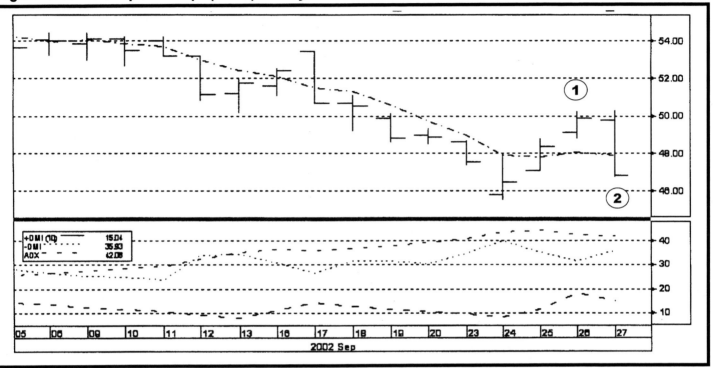

On large first day gains, I will be looking to lock in at least 1/3 (up to 1/2) of my gains when they occur. By doing this, we not only put more in our account, we also lessen our overnight risk.

1) Window setup.

2) Lock in at least 1/3 of the gains due to the large move.

Situation 16

Other Time Frames

Figure 5.16—S&P 500 Index (SPX)—Daily

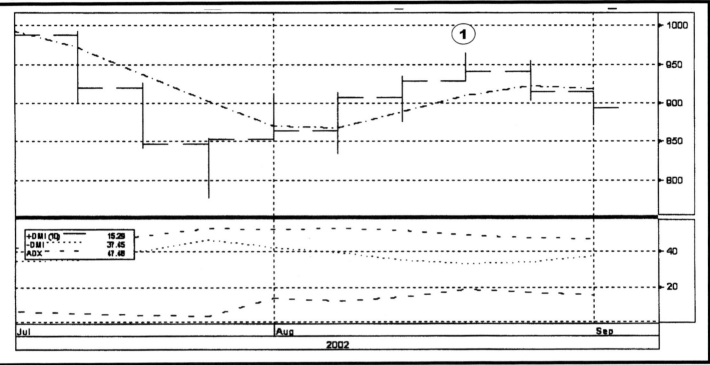

1) Windows work in nearly all time frames. Here is a weekly chart of the S&P 500 which moves 50 points lower in a few weeks. You can trade these setups as 1-3 week moves.

Situation 17

Stop and Re-entry

Figure 5.17—Nasdaq 100 Tracking Stock (QQQ)—Daily

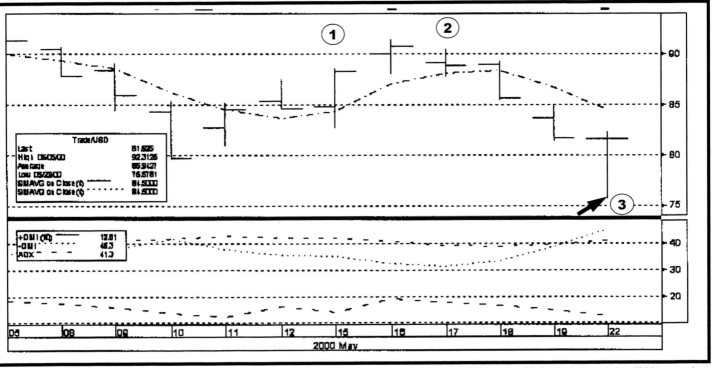

You'll occasionally have situations which will stop you out, but again trigger in a few days. These are many times very good situations.

1) Here is a Window that is stopped out the same day.

2) But you get another chance two days later.

3) For 2 1/2 days this is the perfect Window and when it gets down to 75.50 and starts reversing, you know it's time to lock things in.

Notes

Q&A

I've added some further information here to finalize the knowledge you will need to properly trade the Windows strategy.

Q: It seems that this is a 3-day trade. Is that true?
A: 3 days is the optimal time period. Some trades will only go a few hours and others can go for many days. But, ideally, I want to be locking in profits throughout days 1-3 and sometimes, I'll let it go to day 4. This is purely at your discretion.

Q: Is a 10-period ADX setup better than a 14-period ±DI setup?
A: No. Both are good and combined give ample trading opportunities most trading days.

Q: What if the Window day has a large range? Can I risk less with my stops?
A: Yes, if the range is too big for you, you can tighten the stop to a closer range that you're comfortable with.

Q: Do you have volume requirements?
A: Ideally, you want to stay away from thinly traded stocks. Trade stocks that have at least 100,000 shares traded on average each day.

Q: What happens if there are too many Window setups in one day?
A: This occasionally happens, especially on strongly trending markets, and it's a problem. Ideally, you want to rank the setups as follows:
1. GapWindows
2. HangingWindows
3. DoubleWindows
4. SingleWindows
5. AggressiveWindows

Also, I have found that the bigger the Window, the bigger the snapback when it happens.

Q: It appears that the strategy works in the opposite direction of the longer-term trend. Can I trade it that way too?
A: No! At best, it has a very tiny edge trading in the opposite direction of the trend. But this edge is so small that you have little chance of making long-term money from it and it is not worth the effort expended. **The main reason the strategy works is because reversion to the mean of prices is far stronger when it is taken in the direction of a strong trend.**

Q: How does one go about identifying intraday GapWindows ?
A: The intraday GapWindows are a little tougher to find because you need to have a list of the strongest trending stocks that have Windows from the previous day. Then you must wait to see if they gap, and futher, if that gap gets filled. There is a great deal of non-productive time spent looking for these setups but because they are the strongest Window strategy, I feel it's worth waiting for them to occur.

Q: Is there a simple way to scan for TradingWindows?
A: Depending upon your software program, you can program a scan for the setup.

If you own OmegaResearch's TradeStation, you can order software that looks for the strategy for you (see the back of the book for more information) or you can hire a TradeStation programmer to do it for you.

Q: Is there a recommended position size to trade this strategy?
A: No, only you know how much risk is best for you to take in any given position. My own recommendation is that your position size is large enough to allow you to scale out the position in 3 separate units.

Q: Can you trade Windows in other time frames?
A: Yes, as I showed in the Situation section. Though it does not occur as often, it works equally well on weekly charts.

As you have now seen, this is a very simple, but very powerful strategy. I'll leave you on a final note: The Windows strategy does also many times lead to outsized gains (nearly every month).

For example, while this was being written (September 2002) DKWD and CEY both had very large Window gains. DKWD went from 24 to 11 and CEY went from 29 to 18, both within a few days. Though there is no guarantee these types of moves will occur in the future, as they have in the past. And they have had these moves because they take into account two very strong market principles: trend and price reversion to the mean. When you have these two principles combined, you create the increased probability of finding high percentage moves that many times are substantial.

For example:

The TradingWindows Strategy

Figure 6.1—Certegy Inc. (CEY)—Daily

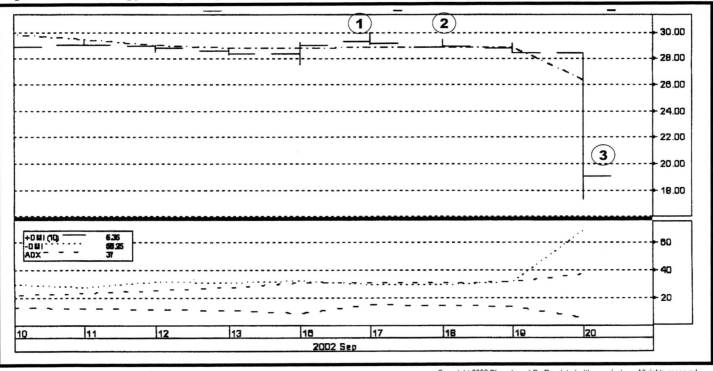

1) Window.

2) Sell short.

3) Collapse.

Figure 6.2—D&K Healthcare Resources (DKWD)—Daily

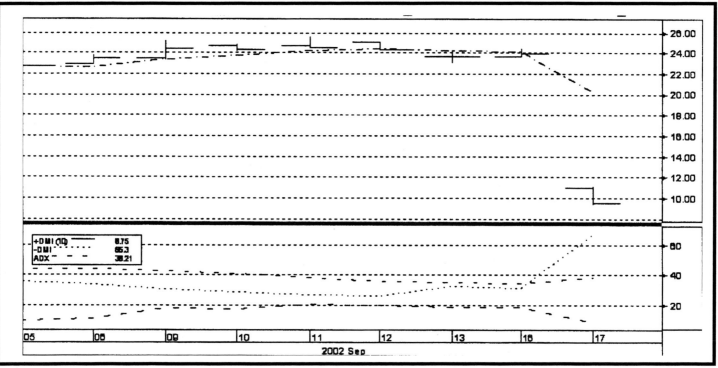

Copyright 2002 Bloomberg LP. Reprinted with permission. All rights reserved.

I was not in this trade but someone I mentored on this strategy was. Gains like this can be found throughout the year and many times happen in the direction of the trend. In this example, the short sale was a bit above 24 and as you can see a few days later, the stock closed under 10.

Notes

Conclusion

As you have seen, this is a simple strategy to identify but it does have many variations and nuances to it. You will find that the more you master these variations and nuances, the more likely you will be able to maximize the profitability of the strategy.

Good luck trading the Windows strategy. If you have any questions or need any help, please email me at lconnors@tradingmarkets.com.

Notes

APPENDIX

Please find helpful information about products and services on the following pages. Please note that these products and services can help you apply the trading strategies you learned in this book more efficiently and greatly enhance your trading results. If you have any further questions, please feel free to call us toll-free at 1-800-797-2584 x1 or email us at andy@mgordonpub.com.

Would You Like To Learn From Larry Connors How To Capture Moves Like These?

10/15/02 - S collapses 11.85 points in 2 days!
09/18/02 - CEY plunges 9.89 points in 3 days!
11/08/02 - LMT implodes 5.91 points in 3 days!
09/12/02 - DKNY collapses 14.49 points in 4 days!
11/08/02 - NOC drops 8.12 points in 3 days!

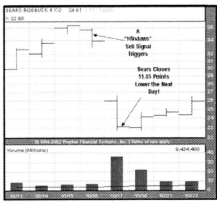

There Is Only One Strategy In The World That Predicted Each Of These Moves. What Is This Strategy? The Connors Windows Strategy!

This is the only strategy that TradingMarkets CEO Larry Connors now uses to short-term trade equities.
And now, for the very first time, you can be taught Larry's Windows Strategy on the very same training module he used to train his private trader!

Dear Fellow Trader,

Each of the above explosive trades was recently taken by Larry Connors, or a trader directly trained by him. Each came from one of Larry's most powerful and simple-to-learn strategies…his Windows strategy. Now, for the first time, you can learn this exact strategy on a bar-by-bar basis directly from your home!

What Is A Connors Window?

A Connors Window is a 1-4 day trade which pinpoints sharp market moves that occur off of pullbacks in a strongly trending market. In this training module, Larry teaches you how to find moves like the ones above.

What Will I Learn From The Connors' Training Module?

First, Larry will teach you the five types of Windows. These are GapWindows, HangingWindows, AggressiveWindows, DoubleWindows and SingleWindows. These five Windows are the base of the entire methodology.

Then, you will be taken into Larry's Training Module and be drilled by Larry on a bar-by-bar basis. As you progress through the module, you will be taught how to trade the Windows Strategy. You will also be taught advanced window techniques and strategies which are being made public for the first time. **These strategies and techniques include:**

- **How to capture the most powerful portion of any rally using Larry Connors' First Windows** – No doubt you have witnessed time and time again how the initial stage of a rally is often the most explosive. Once you have learned Larry's technique of First Windows, you will be able to easily find them and trade these high-velocity moves on a daily basis. You only have to witness how Pixar (PIXR) exploded higher off its Nov. 11 "First Window Pullback," to understand the power of these moves.

- **How to be in great intraday moves, trading the E-minis and SPYs.** Now you'll identify them consistently with The Windows Strategy – For the very first time, Larry Connors has published a methodology to daytrade the E-Minis and SPYs, combining Windows with the VIX. This strategy will allow you to trade intraday market reversals that many times explode in movement.

- **Learn the key to long-term trading success...Trade Management – This is critical!** For those of you who are familiar with Larry's Weekly Battle Plan piece published on TradingMarkets.com, how you execute once you enter a trade is more important than anything else. Obsessive focus on trade management is the major theme of this training module. After you have learned the setups directly from Larry, you will be walked through trade after trade on a bar-by-bar basis, making buy and sell decisions. After you make these decisions, Larry's in-depth analysis will be provided to you to assure that you are managing the trade as perfectly as possible.

When you have completed this training module, you will have a stronger understanding of how to properly manage a trade. You will also be able to leverage this knowledge to all other strategies and trade better than you have in your entire trading career!

Order Larry Connors' Windows Training Module Today!

The cost of the Connors Windows module is $395 and includes complete instructions on how to fully master the strategy. Also included are never-before-published advanced strategies and techniques on how to identify and correctly manage a Windows trade. **Order today and you will receive both online access and the CD-ROM version of Larry's training module.**

Go to www.TradersGalleria.com or call toll-free 1-888-484-8220 x1 and you will soon have Larry Connors coaching you on how to use one of his most powerful trading strategies!

Past results are not indicative of future gains. There is a risk of loss in trading.

Receive *TradingWindows* Setups Nightly and Improve Your Trading Results Immediately!

Specific Setups and Commentary Provided by Laurence Connors Every Day!

You have seen the power of the TradingWindows strategy, now apply it in your own trading. Sign up today and see for yourself how these signals can dramatically change your stock and commodity trading results!

❑ Yes, I would like to start using *The TradingWindows Trading Service* to help me trade the market every day! Please sign me up for the subscription I marked below.

❑ **$150/Month**—By checking this box, filling out and sending in the order form below, I will receive *The TradingWindows Trading Service* for only $150 per month! This service will be billed automatically to my account every month until I cancel.

❑ **$995/Year**—By checking this box, filling out and sending in the order form below, I will receive *The TradingWindows Trading Service* for only $995 per year.

Name: _____

Address: _____

City: _____

Visa/MC/Amex & Exp (mm/yy): _____

Phone: _____

Username/Password: _____

State, ZIP: _____

Email: _____

To Order Call 1-800-797-2584 x1
Or
Sign up online at www.mgordonpub.com
Or
Fill out the order form and fax it to 1-213-955-4242
Or
Fill out this order form and mail it with a check or money order to:
M. Gordon Publishing Group, Inc.

445 S. Figueroa St., Ste. 2930, Los Angeles, CA 90071

Scan For TradingWindow Opportunities Nightly With Your Omega Research TradeStation or SuperCharts Program!

Now, you can scan for TradingWindows setups nightly using your Omega Research TradeStation or SuperCharts program using this powerful new add-on module. Fill out and send in the form below today and see for yourself how these signals can dramatically improve your stock and commodity trading results!

❏ Yes, I would like to start using *The TradingWindows Software Add-on Module* to help me trade the market every day! Please bill my credit card I have listed below for $150 (plus s&h plus applicable taxes) and send me *The TradingWindows Software Add-on Module* immediately!

Name: _____ Phone: _____

Address: _____ Username/Password: _____

City: _____ State, ZIP: _____

Visa/MC/Amex & Exp (mm/yy): _____ Email: _____

To Order Call 1-800-797-2584 x1
Or
Sign up online at www.mgordonpub.com
Or
Fill out the order form and fax it to 1-213-955-4242
Or
Fill out this order form and mail it with a check or money order to:
M. Gordon Publishing Group, Inc.

445 S. Figueroa St., Ste. 2930, Los Angeles, CA 90071

More Trading Books and Software from Laurence A. Connors are available now at www.mgordonpub.com or Call Toll-Free 1-800-797-2584 x1

Trading Connors VIX Reversals

By Laurence A. Connors and Gregory J. Che

Predict The S&P's Direction Up To 68% of The Time! Here is Larry Connors' first published research in over three years. In this just-released guide, you will learn 10 strategies to trade the VIX. Five of these strategies have never been published before! Over the past 8 1/2 years, Connors VIX Reversals have correctly predicted the direction of the S&Ps approximately 65% of the time within a two- to three-day period. Some of these indicators have correctly predicted the market direction nearly 70% of the time!

From this book, you will learn...

- New CVR strategies that are even better than the originals. As powerful as the original signals were, these new signals have pushed the envelope...with some performing with nearly 70% accuracy.

- Trading market sentiment? As you know, the VIX is one of the best ways to measure market sentiment. But no one has ever measured and quantified the VIX the way Connors and Che do.

- To trade mechanically and objectively. $100,000 grew to over $1.9 million in 8 1/2 years by trading CVR signals with these methods.

- SPECIAL BONUS! Included in this manual is Connors' 20-minute audiotape in which he further explains to you how to best trade the CVR signals.

Through both back-testing and actual use in trading, the Connors VIX Reversals have proven to be one of the premier market-timing tools for serious S&P traders, options traders and stock traders. Put this new research to use in your trading today!

100 Pages $100

Trading Connors VIX Reversals Add-on Module for Omega Research TradeStation and SuperCharts Users

By Gregory J. Che

Take command of the scanning and analysis capabilities of your TradeStation or SuperCharts software today with this add-on module based on Larry Connors' latest Connors VIX Reversal (CVR) market timing strategies. This add-on will allow you to scan for trading opportunities daily and intraday based on the CVR 6 through 11 strategies. Simply add-on these professionally programmed indicators into your TradeStation or SuperCharts software using either the PowerEditor or QuickEditor, and you can be up and running in minutes! The systems and indicators in this add-on module provide you with long and short signals, on-chart signal icons and specific entry and exit points. If you own TradeStation or SuperCharts and are looking for a convenient, tested set of strategies to time the markets, buy this add-on module today and capture market sentiment within seconds every day! Includes installation instructions and descriptions of how each indicator and system functions. Individual strategy descriptions are available separately in the trading manual, *Connors on Trading the VIX*.

1-3.5" Diskette and User's Manual $150

Connors on Advanced Trading Strategies

By Laurence A. Connors

If you trade Futures, Stocks or Options, you can now have in your hands 259 pages of the very best material Larry Connors has ever researched, tested and revealed! In 259 pages and 31 chapters, you will learn some of the most explosive short-term market strategies ever made available to traders.

- **Larry Connors has co-authored two of the best-selling trading books of the 1990s.** His first book, *Investment Secrets of a Hedge Fund Manager* (with Blake Hayward) taught traders numerous new strategies that are now in the mainstream of Wall Street. His next book, *Street Smarts* with Linda Raschke, revealed the in-depth secrets of two successful traders. Now, he has released *Connors on Advanced Trading Strategies*, 259 pages for futures, equities and options traders.

- **Easy To Understand.** *Connors on Advanced Trading Strategies* is clearly written and simple to understand. Larry walks you through the rules and combines them with more than 100 charts and examples throughout the book. You will be able to learn and trade these strategies immediately!

You will be taught some of the most explosive short-term strategies available to traders.

Among the 30 plus strategies you will learn are:

- **Connors VIX Reversals I, II, and III (Chapter 2)** - Three of the most powerful strategies ever revealed. You will learn how the CBOE OEX Volatility Index (VIX) pinpoints short-term highs and lows in the S&Ps and the stock market. The average profit/trade for this method is among the highest Larry has ever released.

- **The 15 Minute ADX Breakout Method (Chapter 20)** - Especially for day-traders! This dynamic method teaches you how to specifically trade the most explosive futures and stocks every day! This strategy alone is worth the price of the book.

- **Options (Section 5)** - Four chapters and numerous in-depth strategies for trading options. Learn the strategies used by the best Market Makers and a small handful of professionals to consistently capture options gains!

- **Crash, Burn, and Profit (Chapter 11)** - Huge profits occur when stocks implode. In the past, the Crash, Burn and Profit strategy shorted Centennial Technologies at 49 1/8; six weeks later it was at 2 1/2! It shorted Diana Corp. at 67 3/8; a few months later it collapsed to 4 3/8! It also shorted Fine Host at 35; eight weeks later the stock was halted from trading at 10! This strategy will be an even bigger bonanza for you in a bear market.

- **Advanced Volatility Strategies (Section 2)** - Numerous, never-before-revealed strategies and concepts using volatility to identify markets immediately before they explode.

... and much, much more!

If you are looking for tested, proven day-trading and short-term trading strategies, this manual is for you.

259 Pages Hardcover $150

Street Smarts: High Probability Short-Term Trading Strategies
By Laurence A. Connors and Linda B. Raschke
BEST SELLER - NOW IN ITS 6TH PRINTING!
"Four out of four stars...Excellent!"

    Commodity Traders Consumer Report

If you trade Stocks or Commodities, *Street Smarts* is for you! Linda Raschke and Larry Connors reveal their most successful short-term trading secrets.

Written by Larry Connors and New Market Wizard Linda Raschke, this 242-page manual is considered by many to be one of the best books written on trading futures. Twenty-five years of combined trading experience is divulged as you will learn 20 of their best strategies.

Among the methods you will be taught are:

- **Swing Trading**–The backbone of Linda's success. Not only will you learn exactly how to swing trade, you will also learn specific advanced techniques never before made public.
- **News**–Among the strategies revealed is an intraday news strategy they use to exploit the herd when the 8:30 A.M. economic reports are released. This strategy will be especially appreciated by bond traders and currency traders.
- **Pattern Recognition**–You will learn some of the best short-term setup patterns available. Larry and Linda will also teach you how they combine these patterns with other strategies to identify explosive moves.
- **ADX**–In our opinion, ADX is one of the most powerful and misunderstood indicators available to traders. Now, for the first time, they reveal a handful of short-term trading strategies they use in conjunction with this terrific indicator.
- **Volatility**–You will learn how to identify markets that are about to explode and how to trade these exciting situations.
- Also included are chapters on trading the smart money index, trading Crabel, trading gap reversals, a special chapter on professional money management, and many other trading strategies!

245 PAGES HARDCOVER $175

How Would You Like To Be On The Same Side As The Specialists When They Make The Majority Of Their Money?

Introducing Larry Connors' New Video Course
Buy The Fear, Sell The Greed: Timing the Market Every Day for the Rest of Your Life

In his new video course, Larry Connors will teach you how to trade using his best market-timing strategies for identifying sharp (and often violent) reversals. Larry will teach you his 20 extensively researched and proven timing models (9 of which have never been made public before), plus how to combine them into one super market-timing matrix that gives you a high-probability bias on market direction for the upcoming day. Many times, you will be buying along with the specialists near market bottoms and selling/shorting with the specialists near market tops. This remains one of the biggest edges traders have available to them and now you can learn how it is done!

Here Is What You Will Learn From Larry's Just-Released Video Course:

Section I: Buy the Fear, Sell the Greed—Here's How The Professionals Do It
Larry will teach you the underlying philosophy and logic of his market-timing models. You will develop the confidence needed to execute the trade when buy and sell signals are triggered—even when the rest of Wall Street is telling you to do the opposite.

Section II: Applying The Market-Timing Strategies To Your Trading—Especially For Stock and S&P/E-Mini Traders
In this section, Larry will show you how to apply his 20 best market-timing strategies. Included will be the Connors VIX Reversals (CVRs) 1 through 14, 4 Market Reversal Strategies, and 2 TRIN strategies. Of these, 9 strategies have never been disclosed publicly before. In addition to gaining an intimate understanding of each of these strategies, you will gain these valuable insights—available only in Larry's course among other valuable trading strategies—the single most powerful CVR signal. When this signal is triggered (approximately 20 times a year), this knowledge will enable you to swiftly, precisely and unhesitatingly pounce on the potentially huge move to come.

Section III: The Real Holy Grail...Never Trade Without It!
Before being taught how to put the entire game plan together, Larry will provide you with the one key that is essential for lifetime trading success: proper risk control. Larry will teach you the essential rules of money management, including stops, trailing stops, and profit-taking. You will learn among several other things, Larry's best strategy for taking profits. Larry will teach you one of the best money management strategies ever devised. This approach, properly executed, turns any profitable trade into a free trade. You are able to let your profits run—but do so stress-free because you have sold off part of your position to pay for all its initial cost.

Section IV: Buy The Fear, Sell The Greed - Putting It Into Play
The best part of all this knowledge is that every day, in less than 30 seconds, you will be able use the Connors' Market Timing MATRIX to identify tomorrow's probable market direction. Now, with the Connors' MATRIX, you have the knowledge you need to combine the strengths of all of Larry's market-timing strategies into one powerful indicator. And most of the time, you will be buying in the same direction as the most successful traders in the world—the specialists!

Order this video course today! The cost of the *Buy The Fear, Sell The Greed* video course is $995.00 and includes Larry's 150+ page trading manual teaching you how to be on the same side as the specialists when they make the majority of their money.

P.S. As a special bonus, you will receive **FREE**, a 3 month subscription to Larry's *Nightly Market Timing Service* (a $450 value!). If you already subscribe, 3 months will automatically be added to your subscription. Order your copy today!

150+ PAGE MANUAL AND 8 HOURS OF VIDEO $995

Order Form for M. Gordon Publishing Group, Inc.

To Order Call 1-800-797-2584 x1

Or

Go online at www.mgordonpub.com

Or

Fill out the order form below and fax it to 1-213-955-4242

Or

Fill out this order form and mail it with a check or money order to:

M. Gordon Publishing Group, Inc., 445 S. Figueroa St., Ste. 2930, Los Angeles, CA 90071

Name: _____   Phone: _____

Address: _____   Fax: _____

City: _____   State, ZIP: _____

Visa/MC/Amex: _____   Exp (mm/yy): _____

Qty	Item Name	Price	Total
	Connors/Che: Trading Connors VIX Reversals	$100.00	
	Che: Trading Connors VIX Reversals Add-on Module for Omega Research TradeStation and SuperCharts Users	$150.00	
	Connors: Connors on Advanced Trading Strategies	$150.00	
	Connors: Street Smarts: High Probability Short-Term Trading Strategies	$175.00	
	Connors: Buy The Fear, Sell The Greed Video Course	$995.00	
		Tax (Add 8.25% for CA residents):	
	Shipping (US Mail: $7 + $1 for each add'l item, **Next Business Day**: $17 + $2 for each add'l item, **2 Business Days**: $12 + $2 for each add'l item, **Outside U.S.**: $25 + $5 for each add'l item, **No Shipping Charge for Trading Services**):		
		Grand Total:	

ABOUT THE AUTHOR

Laurence A. Connors is CEO and chairman of TradingMarkets.com. He is also founder and chairman of M. Gordon Publishing Group, a financial markets publishing company. Connors has nearly 20 years experience dealing in the financial markets industry, having started his career in 1981 at Merrill Lynch. In addition to building two companies Larry has also authored a number of top-selling books on trading.